# Beyond the Barline

*Tools for extended phrasing, melodic drumming,*

*And soloing*

## by Chris Munson

## About the Author

Surrounded by music at an early age, Chris Munson grew up listening to, learning from, and performing with some of South Florida's most notable musicians. He got his first drum set at the age of 14 and played his first gig a few weeks later.

After gaining some notoriety in various local music scenes, he decided to try his luck in the Nashville studio scene. For most of the 1990s he actively recorded and performed in Music City. During that time he appeared on over 1,000 recordings, numerous award winning albums (including two Grammy Nominations), toured nationally with a variety of artists, was heard on over 500 radio stations nationwide, and appeared on nationally broadcast television shows and internationally broadcast radio shows. He recorded or performed with several artists including Don Aliquo, David Amram, John Berry, Gail Bliss, Fred Bogert, David Carradine, Bobby Carradine, Vassar Clements, Jeff Coffin, Doug Dillard, Jerry Douglas, Michael Falzarano, Rick Gordon, Wycliffe Gordon, Tom Harrell, Jorma Kaukonen, Lee Konitz, Ronnie McDowell, John McEuen, Leon Medica, Tim O'Brien, Anders Osborne, Greg Osby, Mickey Rafael, LeAnn Rimes, Merl Saunders, Jamey Simmons, Chester Thompson, Trout Fishing in America, and Snooky Young.

Chris holds a B.M. in Percussion Performance from Eastern Kentucky University and a M.A. in Jazz Studies from Middle Tennessee State University. He is currently the Cooridinator of Music Media and Music Business at the University of Louisiana at Lafayette where he teaches courses in audio production, music business, and applied drum set. He is an active composer / arranger in a multitude of genres and his original compositions are published by Drop 6 Media, Tapspace, Simmons Jazz, and Engine Room Publishing.

# Introduction

Playing the drum set is a life-long endeavor that requires focus, agility, discipline, and patience. Regardless of our skill level, most of us encounter the same musical roadblocks as we strive to improve our playing. All too often we are hesitant to acknowledge or endure the difficulties associated with fixing complex musical problems. This is especially true when we listen to drummers we admire, who seem to play with effortless mastery.

What follows in this book should not be viewed as a collection of exercises. Rather, it is an approach to practicing intended to allow you to dissect any musical situation down to its simplest parts and reconstruct it in any form you see fit.

Before I explain the concept of this book and how it is meant to develop your playing, lets look at some common problems many drummers face:

1) Practicing things we already know instead of things that make us uncomfortable.
2) Playing fills that only last one bar.
3) Ending those fills on beat one of the following bar.
4) An inability to use all four limbs with equal prowess.
5) Trouble assimilating various musical styles.
6) Feeling a general lack of creativity.
7) Too focused on music / playing parts correctly that we aren't listening to the band.
8) Playing fills every two and / or four bars but missing fills / kicks at the most crucial musical points.
9) Unable to solo.

Now, when most of us seek to improve our playing or learn something new, we turn to books, videos, magazines, blogs, forums, or private lessons. These things are all valid and of benefit to our playing. However, a common problem I see with this is that it typically leads us to learn scripted grooves / fills or only play exercises. That leaves us with the inability to express what we've learned in our own unique musical language.

The following exercises are intended to help you move beyond some of these creative limitations. They are indeed a collection of exercises, but it is important to view them more as an ***approach to playing***. Once you understand how this approach can deconstruct virtually any musical situation, you will discover how to use it to develop your own 'voice' when playing.

The next time you are behind the drum set, take a moment to think about ***where*** your playing is being generated. Typically you will come to the conclusion that you are playing from your ***mentally, emotionally,*** or ***physically (chops)***. It is difficult to get all three of these sources of our playing to work simultaneously and fluidly. What follows in this book is intended to give you the physical ability to play what you hear or feel the instant you realize it.

## Part One: Two Note Exercises

Let's start by tackling one of the more common musical ticks we exhibit: ***only playing fills one bar in length that end on beat one of the following measure.***

Most drummers are familiar with the concept of playing one time signature **over** another. For example, if you were asked to play 3 over 2, 3 over 4, or 5 over 4, it would be notated as follows:

This works great if you want to imply to different time signatures or feels in a limited space. However, notice that each of these is only a bar (or measure) in length. We are again limited to the framework of the barline.

Now, what if we used the same notational base (in this case 16ths) in two limbs and implied 3 over 4 using accents (or more accurately, 3 **against** 4). Here's what it would look like:

Notice that when we play the 3 vs. 4 feel this way, we get a phrase that is **three bars long**! This allows us to build up some tension with our playing that is ultimately resolved after a short, but odd numbered amount of bars. As we will see a little later on, this type of sonic conflict in our playing adds excitement and interest to the listener by creating something that is a little out of the ordinary.

Below are examples of two note exercises like the one above. These are meant to be primers for the three and four note exercises. These **are not** intended to build chops or enhance sight-reading abilities. They are simply designed to embed the contrasting patterns in your mind / ears and open your eyes to some ways to vary exercises beyond what is written on the page.

If you look closely at many of the exercises you will see contrasting motion between the accent patterns. That is, sometimes the moving pattern (2, 3, 4, 5, 6, or 7) will seem to be racing ahead of or falling behind the pulse pattern. You will also notice this aurally and feel it physically as you begin to immerse yourself in the exercises. Soon you should begin to get a sense of simultaneous push and pull depending on which patterns you are playing.

Remember that these are not sight-reading exercises. I suggest that you 'get your head out of the page' as quickly as possible. It is very important to internalize these patterns so that you can express them in your own musical vocabulary and recall them at will.

Try to work through the following two notes examples in this order:

1) Play as written.
2) Switch accent patterns to opposite hands.
3) Remove the subdivision and play only the accents.
4) Revoice the patterns.
   - Left hand and left foot
   - Right hand and right foot
   - Right hand and left foot
   - Left hand and right foot
   - Both feet
5) Let the hand playing the accent move around the kit freely while the opposite hand stays on one sound source.
6) Let both hands move around the kit freely (one plays moving pattern, one plays base pattern).
7) Both hands play moving pattern and move around kit freely while the feet play base pattern.

As you can see, there are quite a few ways to vary the exercise. This approach to dissecting and reconstructing a musical device will be extremely beneficial to long-term growth in your playing. It is important for you to understand that these are not the only ways to vary the following exercises and that you can tackle any musical problem with this approach.

**2 AGAINST 4**

**3 AGAINST 4**

**4 AGAINST 4**

4 AGAINST 4
VARIATION #2

5 AGAINST 4

## 5 Against 4 Variation 2

## 5 Against 4 Variation 3

8

6 AGAINST 4

6 AGAINST 4
VARIATION 2

9

7 AGAINST 4

7 AGAINST 4
VARIATION #2

7 Against 4
Variation #3

7 Against 4
Variation #4

Here are some brief examples of the variations for these exercises. Though it is completely acceptable to write these out (and I've had many students do so), you will ultimately benefit the most from trying to visualize these variations while looking at the original patterns. I find this aids in performance situations, allowing you to play with confidence and creativity. This also helps you to develop the ability to improvise and 'read between the lines' when you are given a less than desirable drum set chart.

SWITCH ACCENTS
3 AGAINST 4

ACCENTS ONLY
3 AGAINST 4

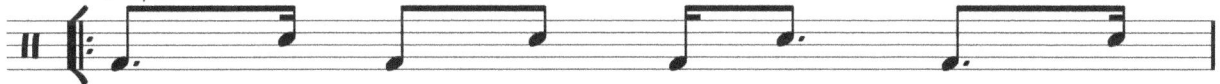

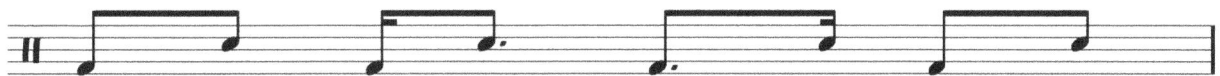

LEFT HAND / LEFT FOOT
2 AGAINST FOUR

RIGHT HAND / RIGHT FOOT
2 AGAINST FOUR

RIGHT HAND / LEFT FOOT
2 AGAINST FOUR

LEFT HAND / RIGHT FOOT
2 AGAINST FOUR

BOTH FEET
2 AGAINST FOUR

The previous examples all had a duple based feel.  If we are to truly expand our playing abilities, we must also explore these exercise in a triple / tuplet based setting.

The following exercises are similar to the previous ones except that they are tuplet based.  Note that even though you are still in 4/4, the base patterns are now in groups of three.  Also keep in mind that we are accenting one grouping *against* another, not *over* it.  So you will find some anomalies in which you are playing one value *against* another but hearing a completely different value *over* another.

Once you complete these exercises, apply the same variations used for the 16th note patterns.

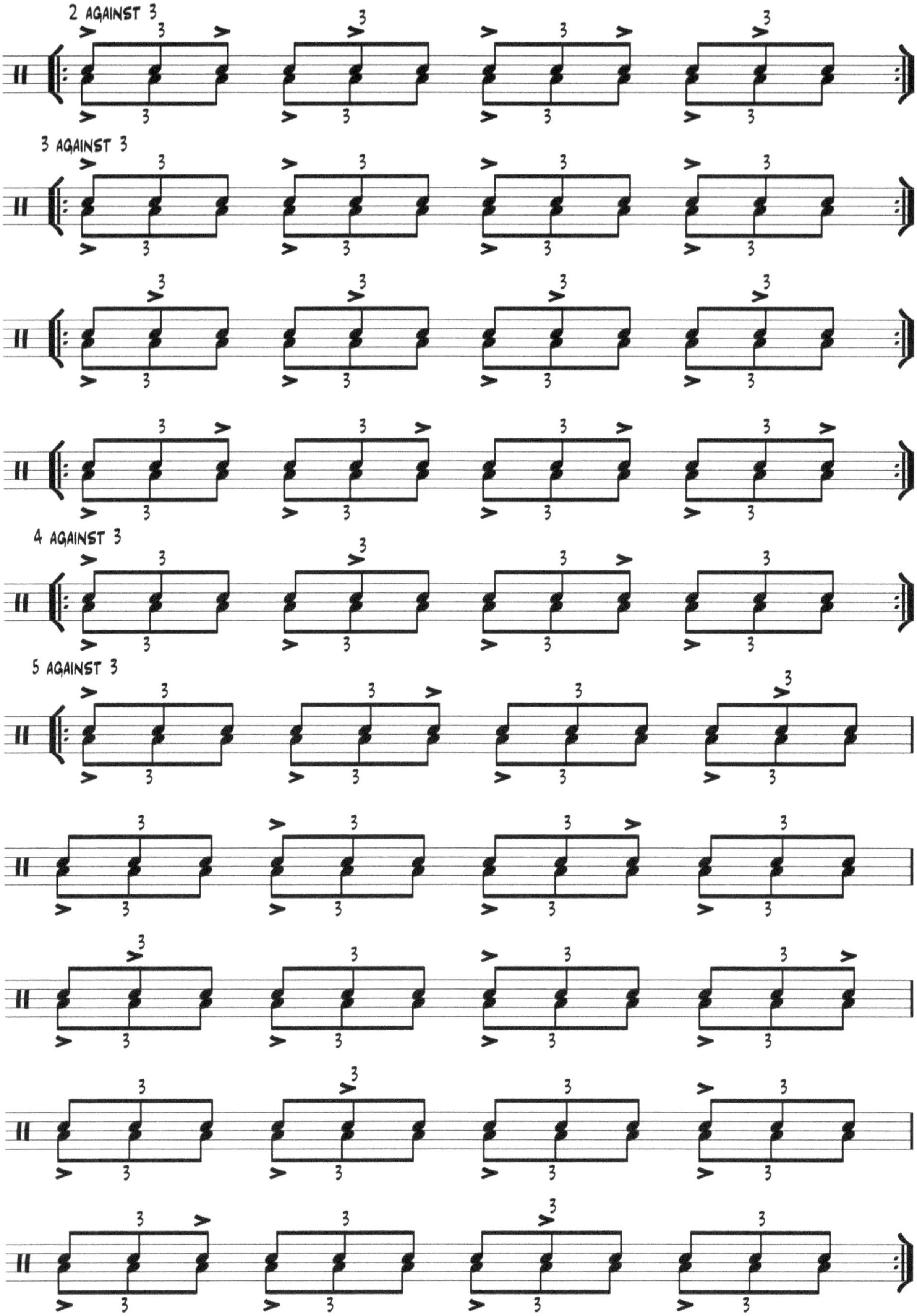
2 AGAINST 3
3 AGAINST 3
4 AGAINST 3
5 AGAINST 3

5 AGAINST 3
VARIATION #2

5 AGAINST 3
VARIATION 3

19

6 AGAINST 3

6 AGAINST 3
VARIATION #2

20

7 AGAINST 3

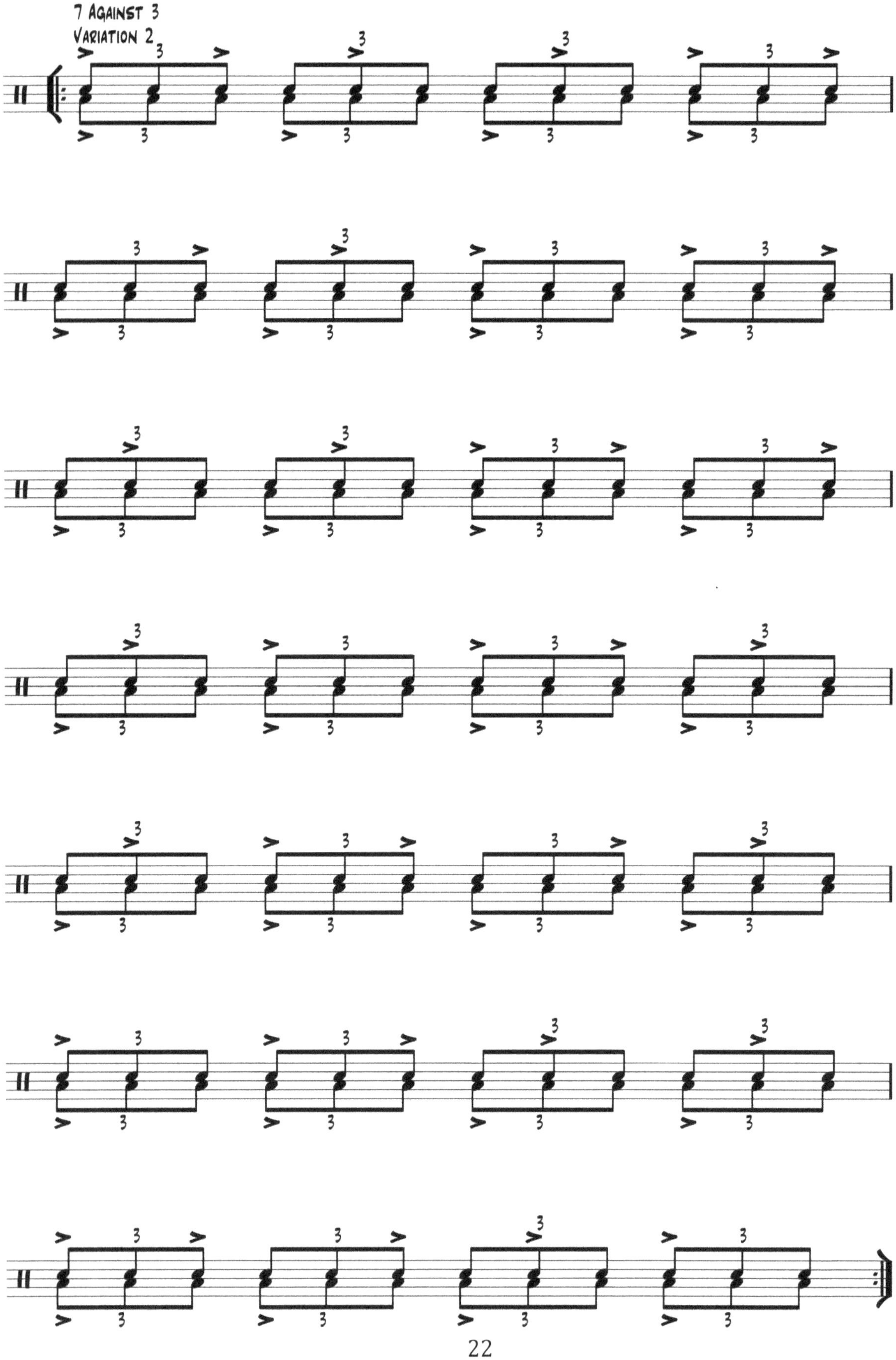
7 Against 3
Variation 2

7 Against 3
Variation 3

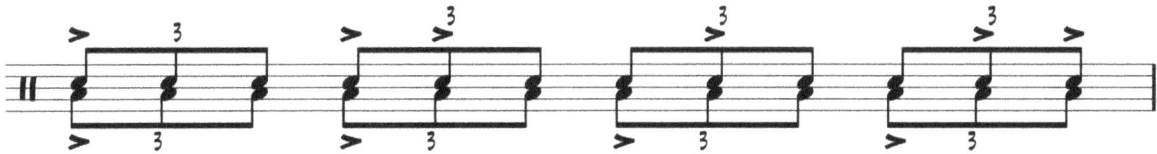

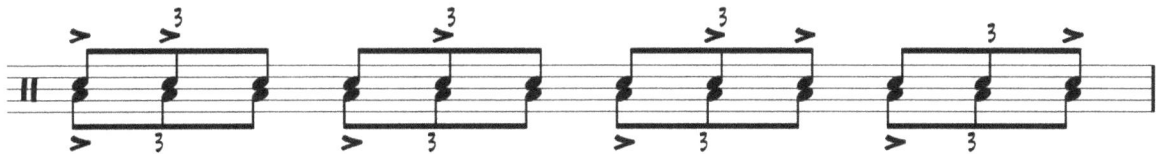

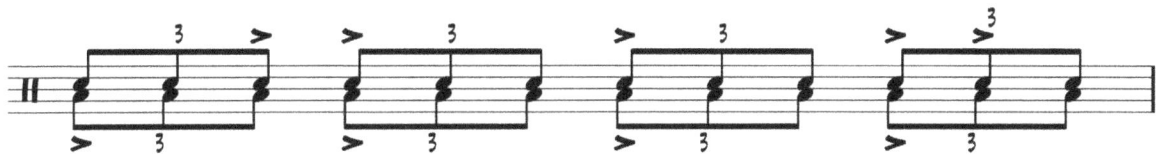

23

7 Against 3
Variation 4

24

## Part Two: Three Note Exercises

Once you have become acclimated with the feeling of playing two accent patterns simultaneously, it is time to add an element of independence to the exercises. You will now play the accent patterns (2, 3, 4, 5, etc.) on the snare drum using a straight sticking (**R L R L R L etc.**). You will also play an ostinato pattern with the kick drum and stepped high hat.

Start simple with something like a four on the floor kick drum / hi hat pattern. This is essentially a one beat pattern that will make it easier for you to concentrate on the moving accent pattern. As you become comfortable, progress to more intricate foot patterns like **Samba, Songo, Second-line,** and **Clave**. These are not the only patterns you can play, but they are some of the more common foot patterns you will encounter when playing live.

The longer the foot pattern the more difficult it becomes to play the moving accent pattern. The idea is to set your feet on autopilot so that you don't have to think about what they are doing.

Here are a few examples of ostinato patterns for the feet:

FOUR ON THE FLOOR

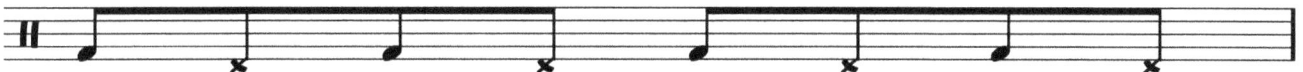

SONGO

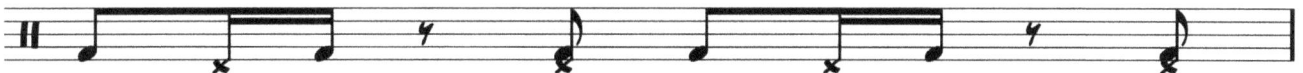

SECOND LINE

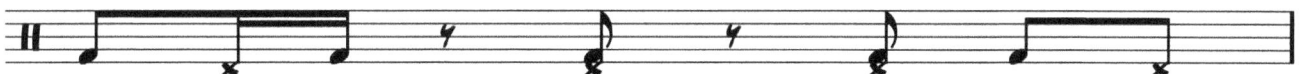

CLAVE

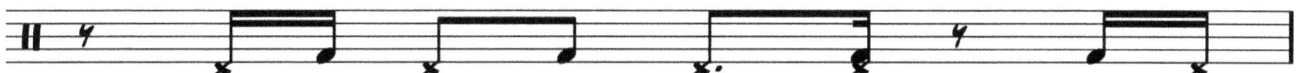

25

As with the two note patterns, these are not intended to be sight-reading exercises. The idea is to set the feet in motion and then basically ignore them while the hands work through the various polyrhythms.

Looking at the exercises in a vertical fashion (how the snare, kick, and hi hat line up) may prove to be frustrating. These exercises focus on a moving line and should be viewed left to right, not up and down. There are some instances where you may need to break the exercise down vertically in order to tackle problematic spots. For the most part, however, you should avoid approaching the exercises in this fashion.

## How to Play the Exercises

Again, resist the urge to play fast. **Sound** and *feel* are the most important aspects of these exercises. Once you achieve a clean sound and solid feel you can move on to accelerating the tempo.

I find it helpful to begin by simply playing the ostinato underneath the unaccented pattern (16th or tuplet). Then begin inserting the accents. When you encounter exercises that are more difficult, it is helpful to add the accents one at a time until you become comfortable with the entire thing.

I suggest you work through the following two notes examples in this order:

1) Play as written.
2) Reverse sticking (L R L R L R etc.).
3) Revoice the patterns.
   - Place the accents on the toms
   - Add double strokes to all non-accented notes
   - Place the accents on cymbals
   - Play the exercises as grooves by moving the right hand to the hi-hat or ride cymbal and leaving left hand on snare. Ghost all non-accented snare notes
   - Play the exercises as groove but use alternative stickings (R L L R L L for example)
4) Improvise! It is important to spend as much time experimenting with these exercises as it is practicing them. Try setting an ostinato in motion and playing freely with the hands around the kit. Often I will let my hands roam around for a while until I accidently play something that I dig. Then I will spend time trying to figure out what just happened so that I can incorporate it into my playing.

# FOUR ON THE FLOOR

5 Against 4

5 Against 4
Variation 2

28

5 AGAINST 4
VARIATION 3

6 AGAINST 4

6 Against 4
Variation 2

6 Against 4
Variation 3

**7 Against 4**

7 Against 4
Variation 2

7 AGAINST 4
VARIATION 3

33

# SONGO

5 AGAINST 4

5 AGAINST 4
VARIATION 2

5 AGAINST 4
VARIATION 3

6 AGAINST 4

6 Against 4
Variation 2

6 Against 4
Variation 3

7 Against 4
Variation 2

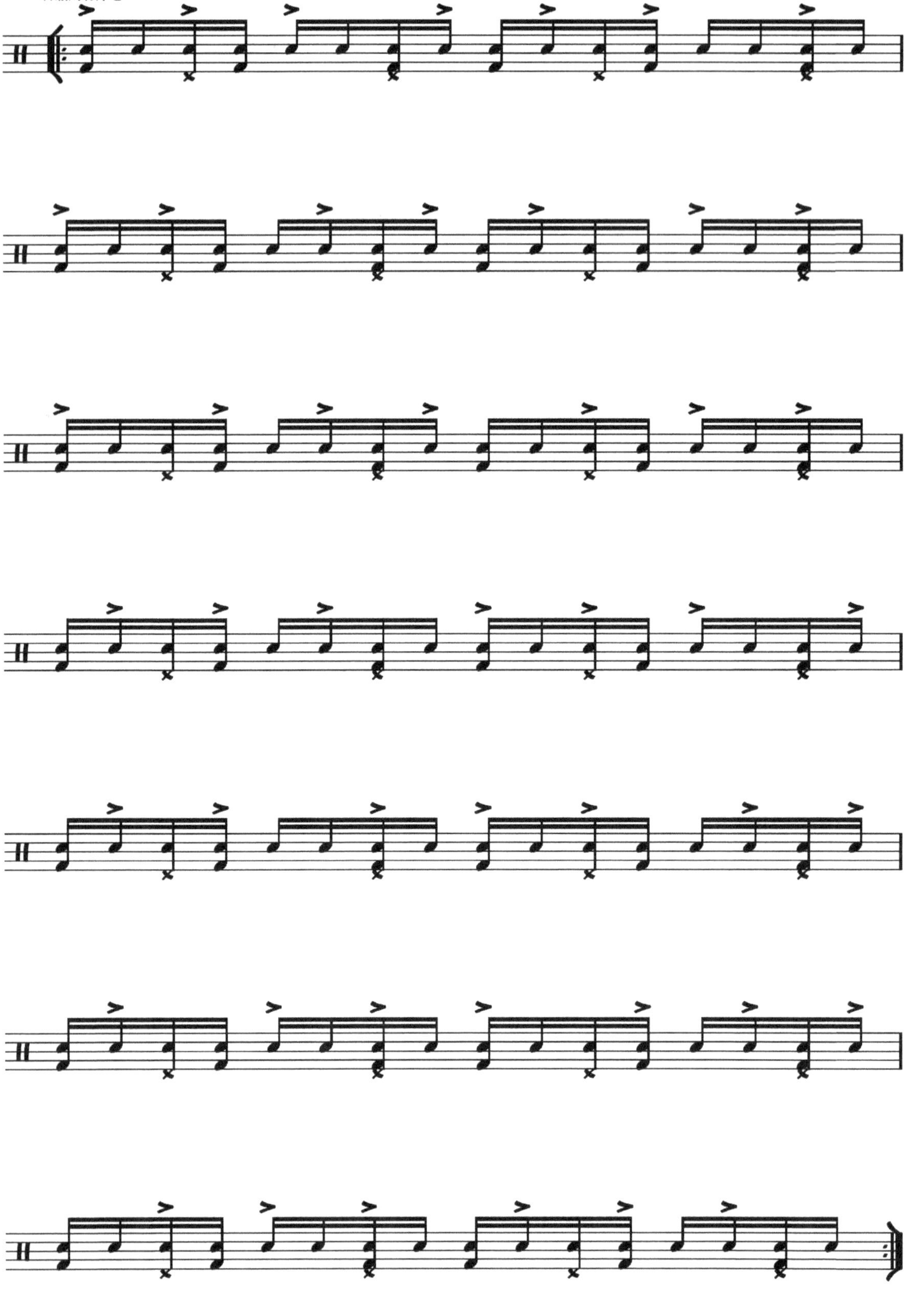

7 Against 4
Variation 3

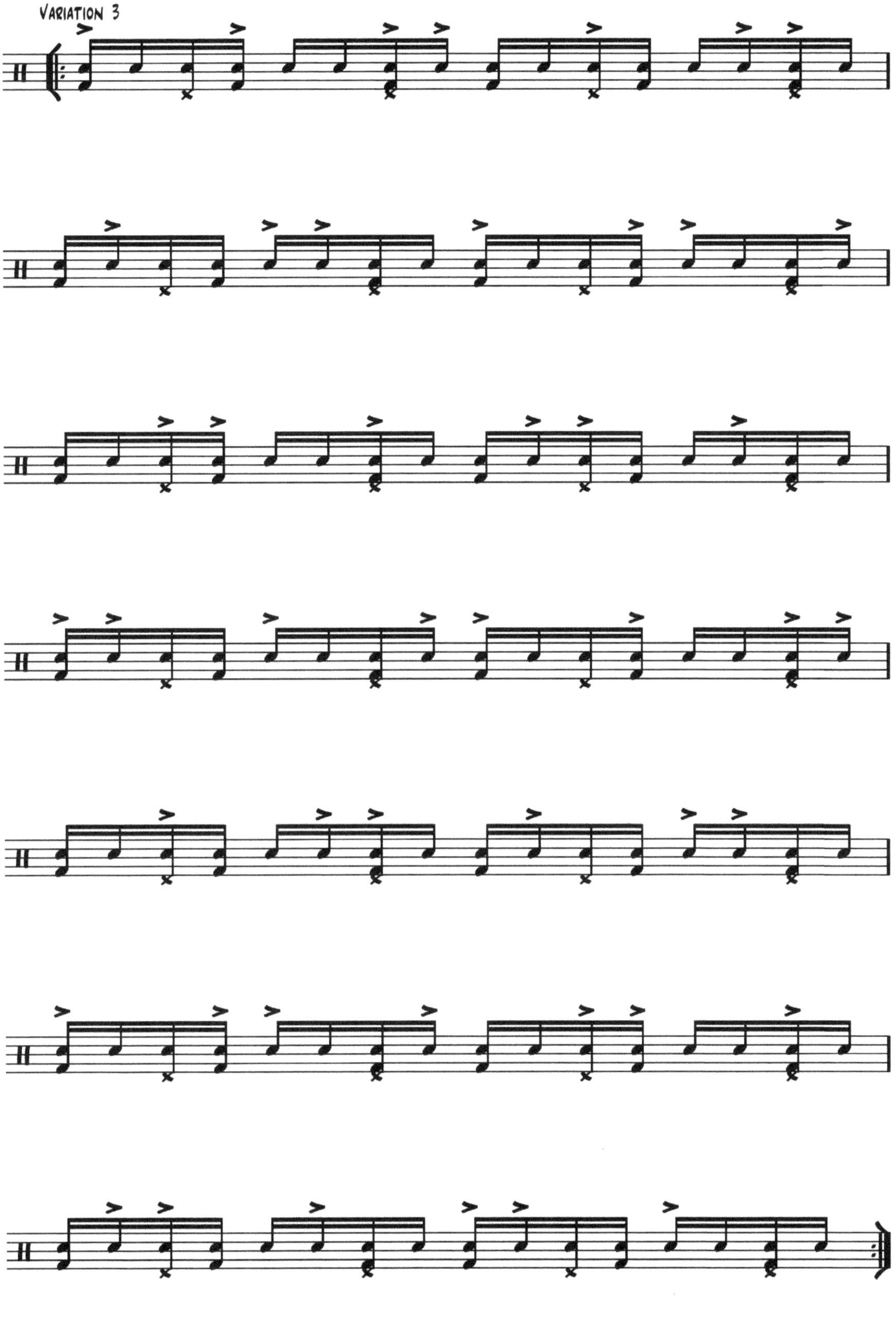

7 Against 4
Variation 4

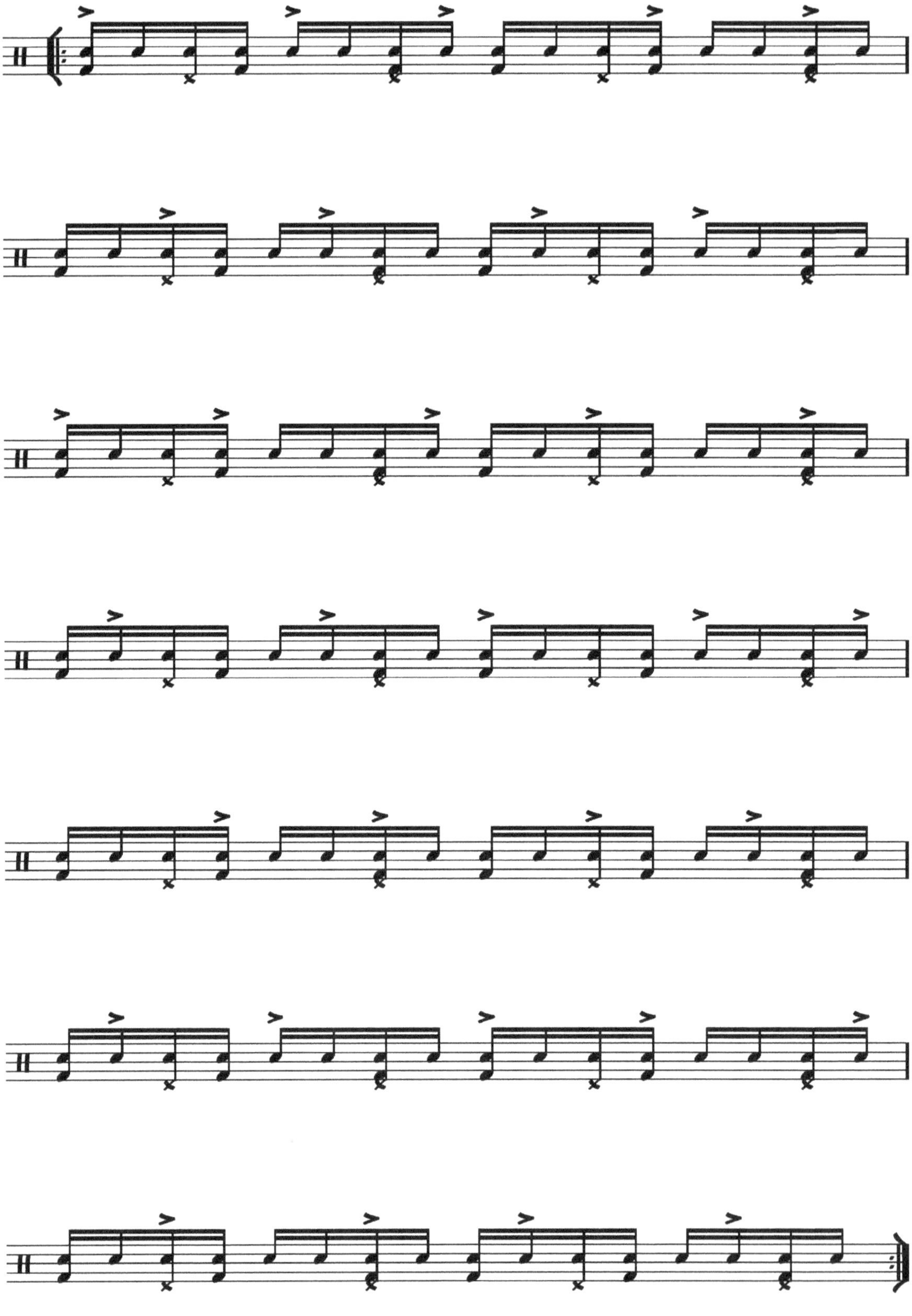

## SECOND LINE

2 AGAINST 4

3 AGAINST 4

4 AGAINST 4

5 AGAINST 4

44

5 AGAINST 4
VARIATION 2

45

5 Against 4
Variation 3

6 AGAINST 4

6 AGAINST 4
VARIATION 2

6 AGAINST 4
VARIATION 3

7 AGAINST 4

**7 AGAINST 4**
**VARIATION 4**

# CLAVE

**2 AGAINST 4**

**3 AGAINST 4**

**4 AGAINST 4**

5 AGAINST 4

54

55

5 Against 4
Variation 3

57

6 AGAINST 4
VARIATION2

7 Against 4

7 Against 4
Variation2

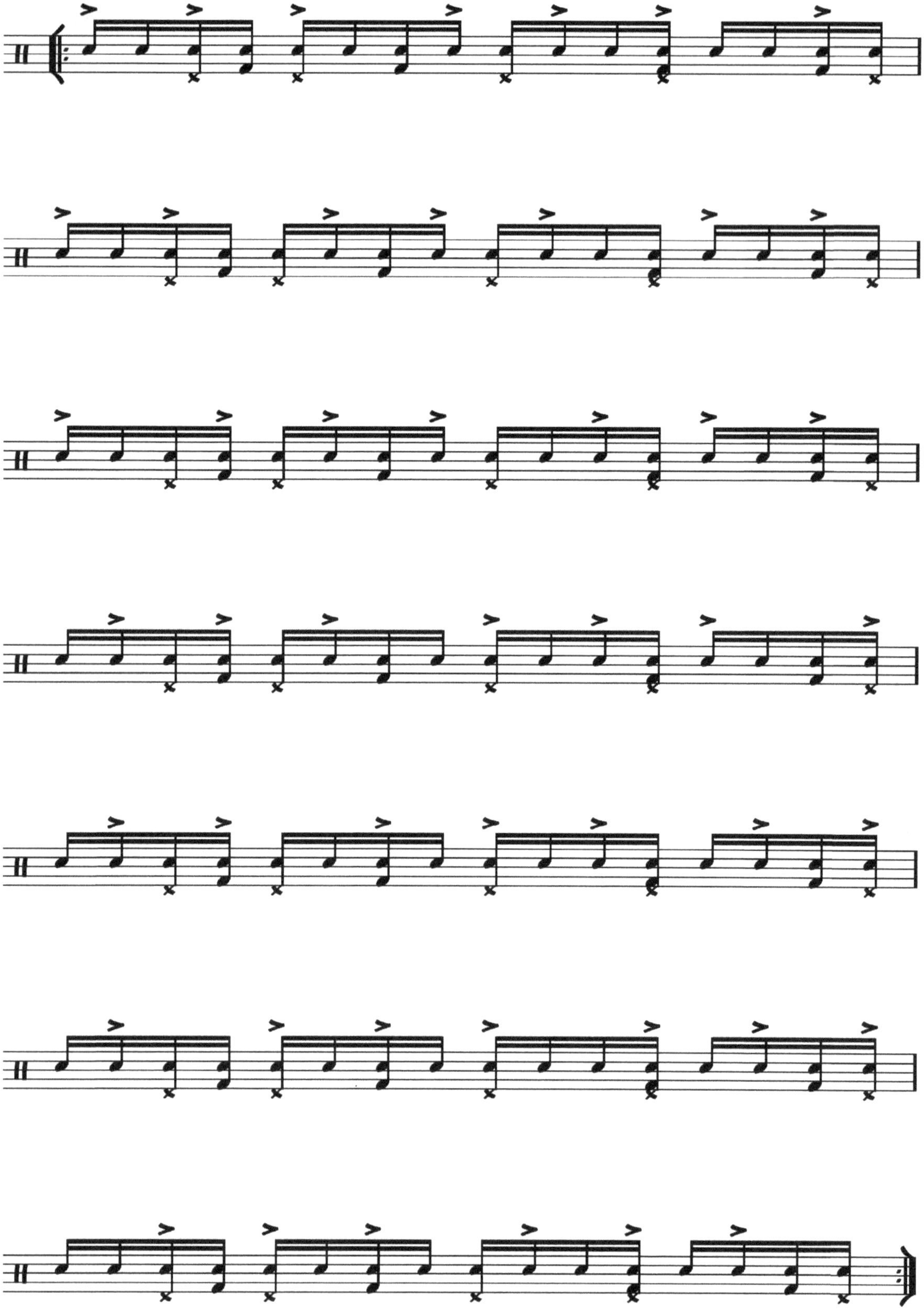

7 AGAINST 4
VARIATION 3

61

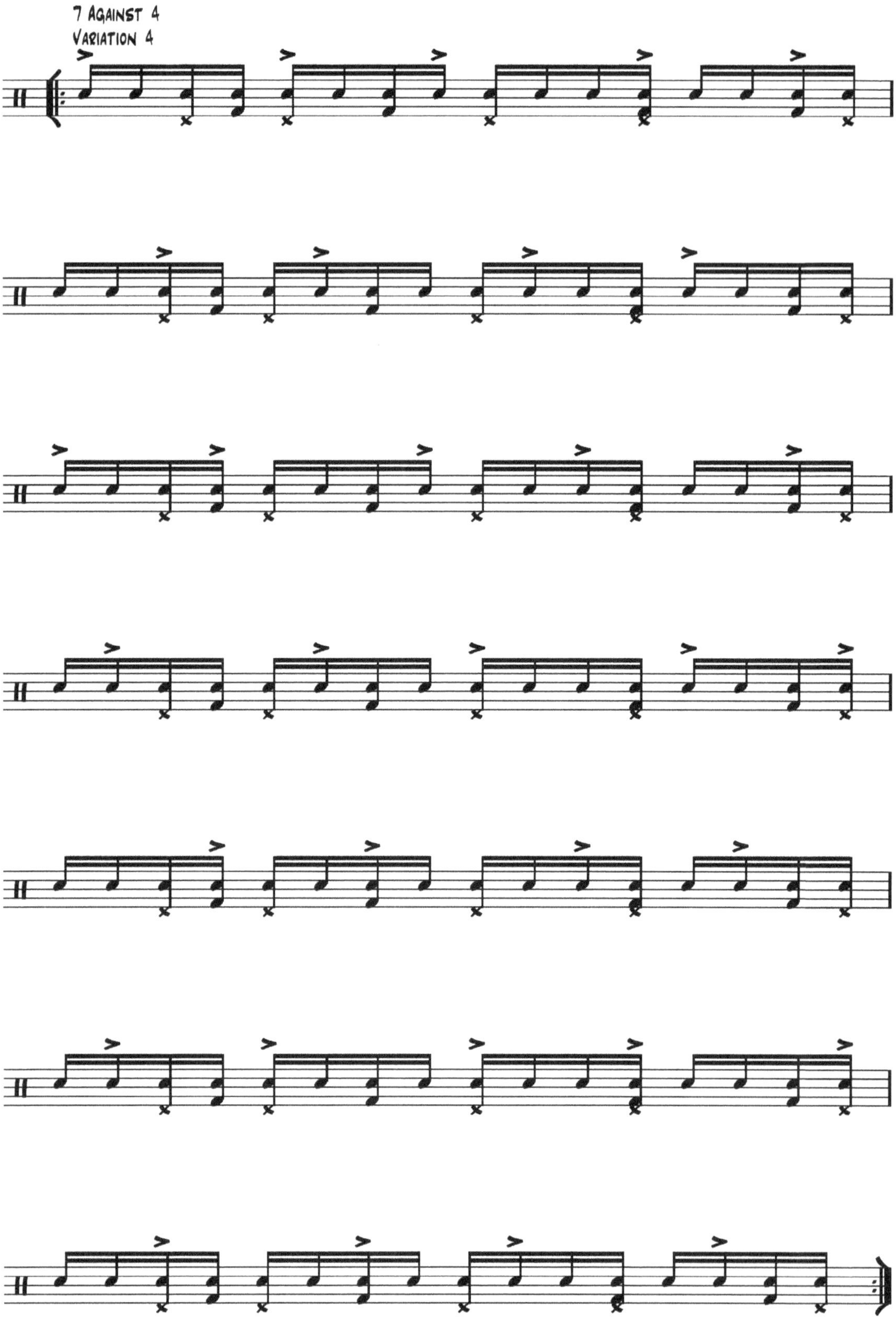
7 Against 4
Variation 4

Here are some examples of variations for the exercises. I personally like to look at the original exercises and visualize the variations. You may find this difficult to do on some of the more complicated variations. If that's the case simply transcribe the variation so you can visually see how it lays out.

**3 Against 4**
**Tombs play accents**

**3 Against 4**
**Tombs play accents**
**Snare plays double strokes**

6 AGAINST 4
ACCENTS ON CYMBALS

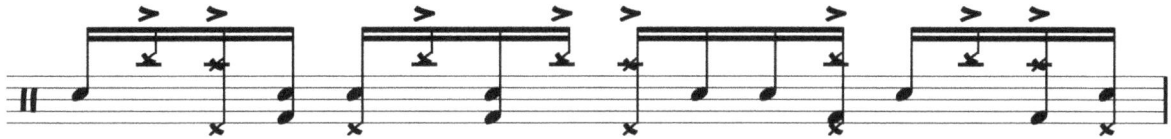

3 AGAINST 4
AS GROOVE

7 Against 4
Alternate Sticking - Paradiddle

66

## Tuplet Subdivision

As with the two-note variation, the accent patterns are also applied using a tuplet feel. The

underlying ostinatos for this section include a basic four on the floor, reggae, and shuffle groove.

Remember, these are only a few of the limitless possibilities.


After you have mastered these exercises, apply the same variations described for the sixteenth

note exercises.

## Four on the Floor

5 Against 3
Variation 2

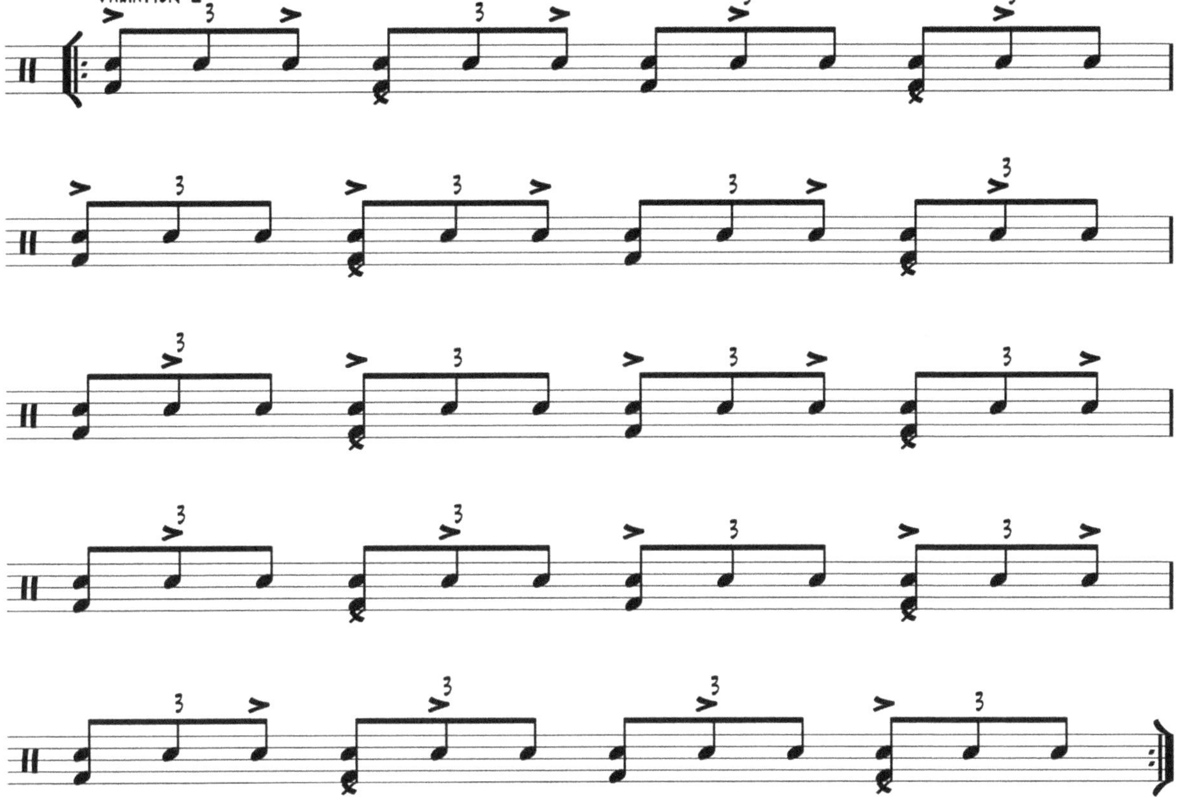

5 Against 3
Variation 3

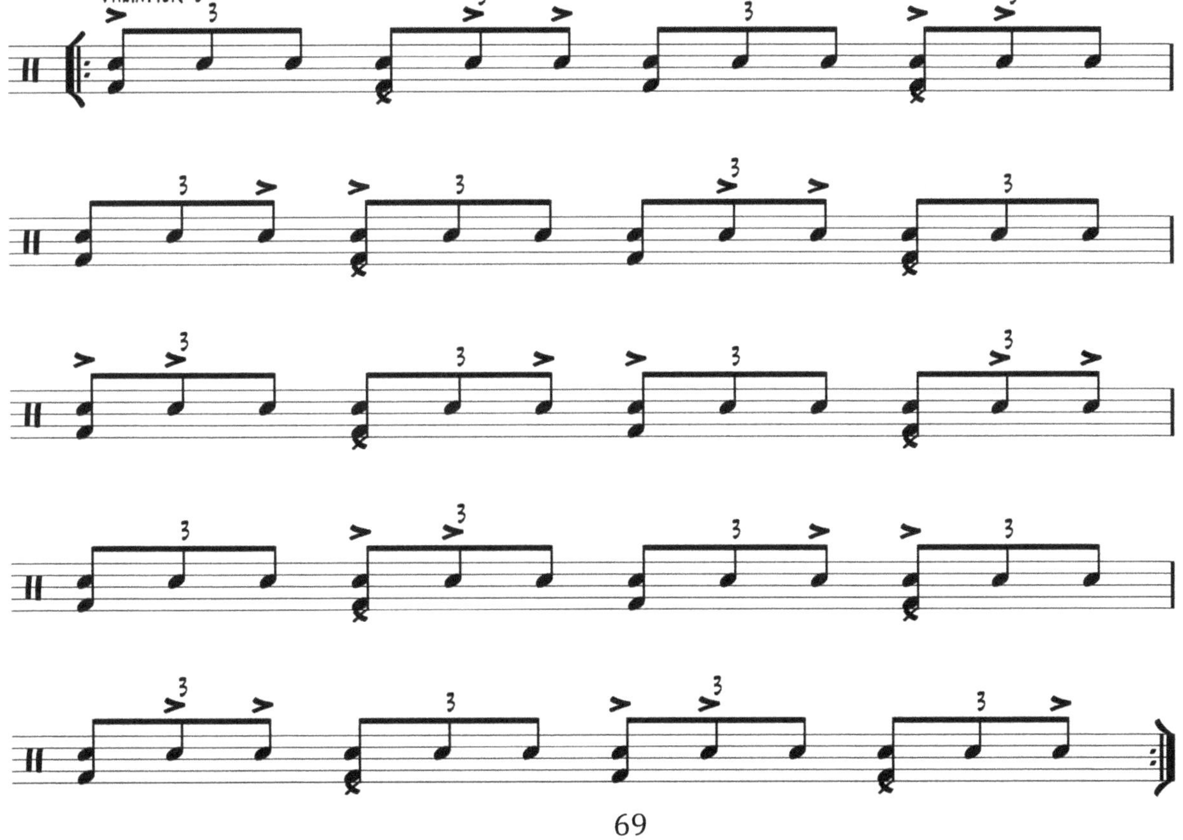

6 Against 3

6 Against 3
Variation 2

7 AGAINST 3

71

7 Against 3
Variation 2

7 Against 3
Variation 3

7 Against 3
Variation 4

74

## REGGAE

5 Against 3
Variation 2

5 Against 3
Variation 3

6 Against 3

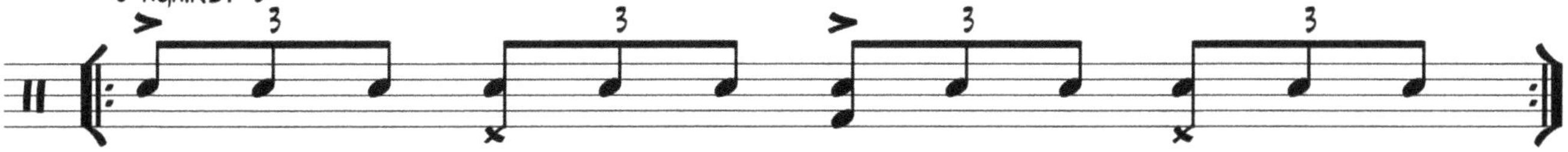

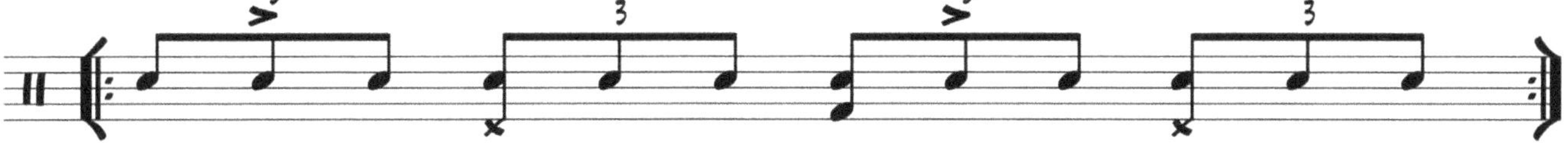

6 Against 3
Variation 2

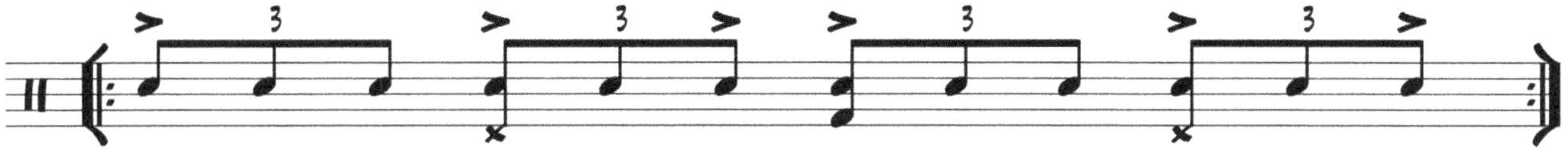

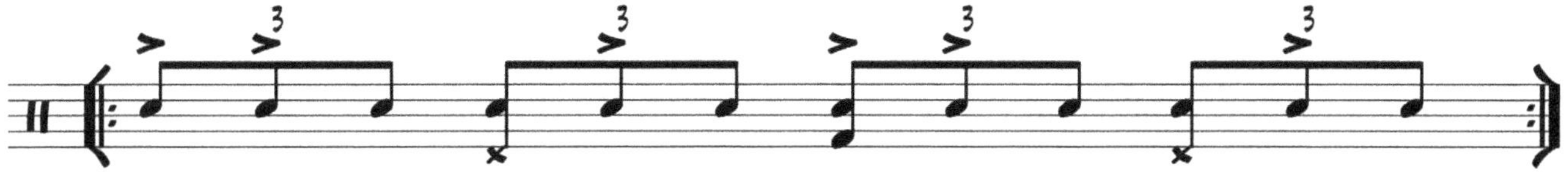

7 AGAINST 3

78

**7 AGAINST 3**
**VARIATION 2**

7 AGAINST 3
VARIATION 3

80

7 Against 3
Variation 4

81

## SHUFFLE VARIATION

82

5 Against 3
Variation 2

5 Against 3
Variation 3

83

6 Against 3

6 Against 3
Variation 2

7 AGAINST 3

7 Against 3
Variation 2

7 Against 3
Variation 3

7 Against 3
Variation 4

# Part 3: Four Note Exercises

It is now time to apply the accent patterns over a three-note ostinato. These exercises are intended to develop four-way independence. You will play an ostinato with the ride cymbal, kick drum, and hi hat while playing the accent patterns on the snare drum. Note that you are now extracting the **accents only** and not playing a steady stream of sixteenths on the snare drum.

The four-note pattern will look something like this:

When the moving line is removed, the ostinato looks like this:

Again, the idea is to set the ostinato in motion and then forget about it. Inevitably you will find some of the ostinato patterns more difficult than the others. I suggest you extract the ostinato first and play it until it feels loose and comfortable. Then begin approaching the exercises.

By now, the accent patterns should be burned into your ears and muscle memory. Try to continue the linear thought process and avoid getting bogged down by how the notes line up vertically. There are times that you may have to work out figures note by note. However, I suggest that you approach problematic passages by playing the ostinato and inserting one accent at a time.

## How to Play the Exercises

I suggest you work through the following two notes examples in this order:

1) Play as written.
2) Revoice the moving line. Try playing the snare part around the kit using the toms, cymbals, or other sound sources.
3) Revoice the moving line and the ride cymbal. While the snare part is moving also move the ride part to various cymbals. Sometimes this can be physically challenging but it also creates interesting textures.
4) Switch parts. Have the snare play the ride cymbal part and vice versa. Or have one of the feet play the moving line. There are several combinations that you can come up with by altering each limb's part.
5) Revoice the snare part utilizing rudiments. For instance, play the moving line around the kit but embed a larger pattern like a paradiddle in the movement. The pattern could be something like HT, SN, LT, SN, HT, SN, HT, SN, LT, etc. Here you would be playing a paradiddle between the toms with the snare drum filling in every other note.
6) Combine patterns. This is extremely difficult and rewarding. Pick four accent patterns and assign one to each limb. You will probably have to write this out as the combinations create elongated patterns and are sometimes difficult to hear.
7) Improvise! Now you have developed an extensive vocabulary to improvise with. Try mixing and matching accents / variations and allowing yourself to develop new ideas.

# FOUR ON FLOOR

**5 Against 4**

5 Against 4
Variation 2

93

5 Against 4
Variation 3

94

6 Against 4
Variation 2

6 Against 4
Variation 3

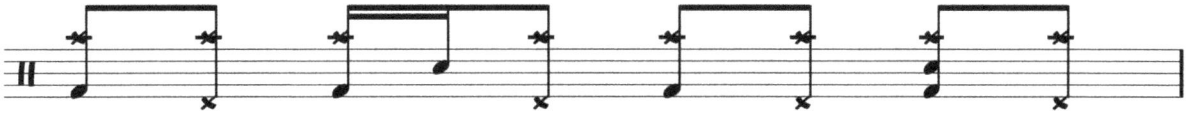

**7 AGAINST 4**
**VARIATION 2**

7 AGAINST 4
VARIATION 4

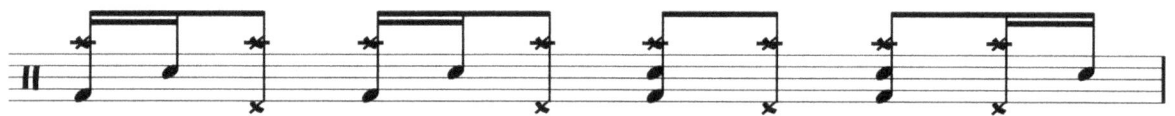

## SONGO VARIATION

**4 Against 4**

**5 Against 4**

5 AGAINST 4
VARIATION 2

5 AGAINST 4
VARIATION 3

103

6 Against 4

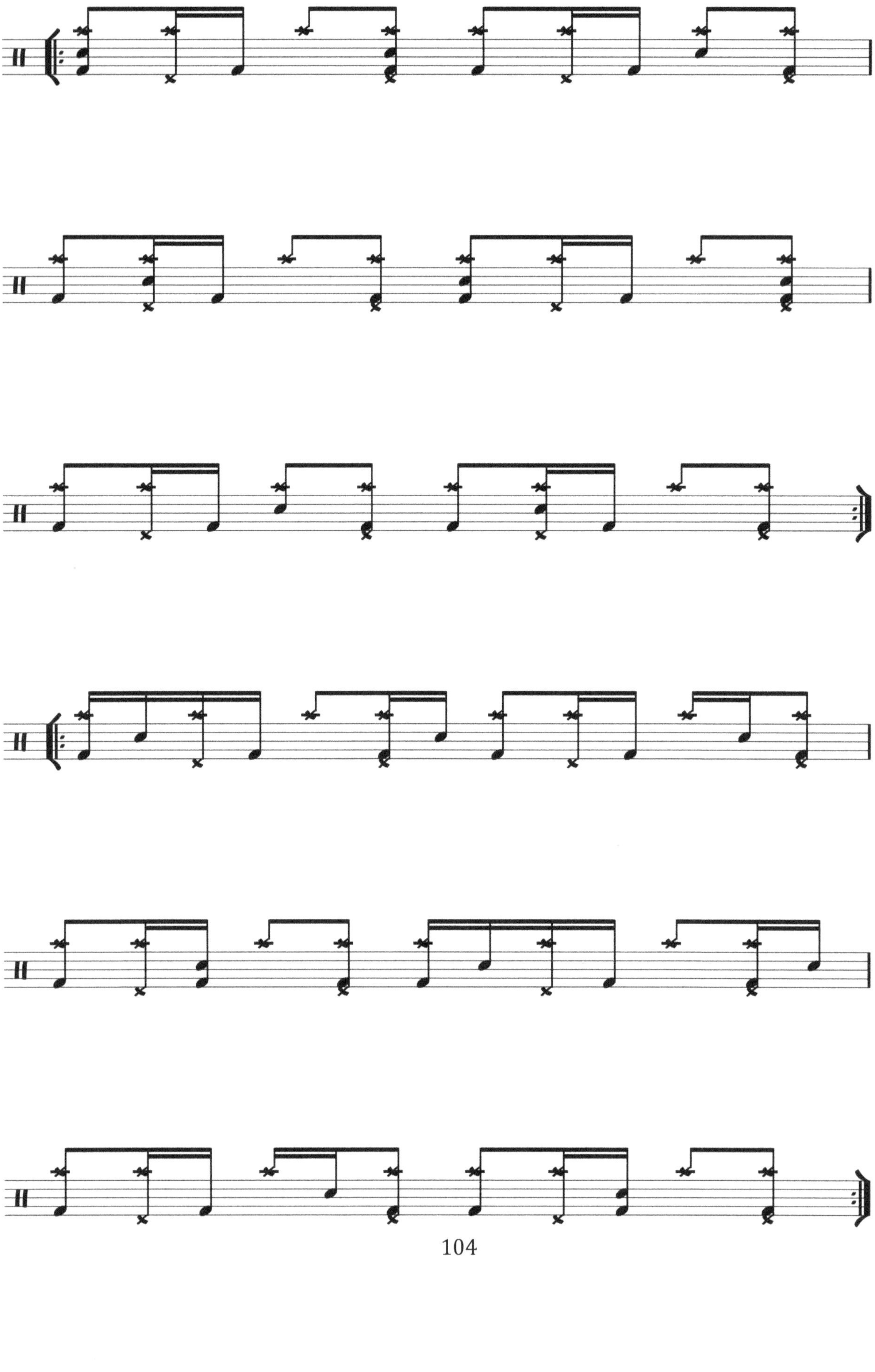

7 Against 4

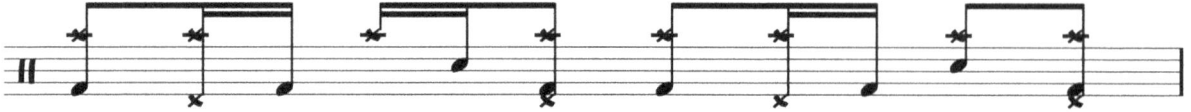

7 AGAINST 4
VARIATION 2

107

7 Against 4
Variation 3

108

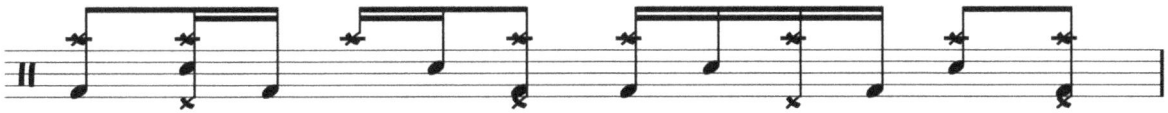

# CLAVE VARIATION

## 2 Against 4

## 3 Against 4

## 4 Against 4

5 Against 4

111

5 Against 4
Variation 2

5 Against 4
Variation 3

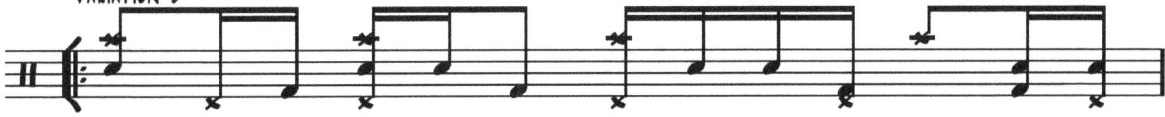

6 AGAINST 4

6 Against 4
Variation2

115

7 Against 4

7 Against 4
Variation2

117

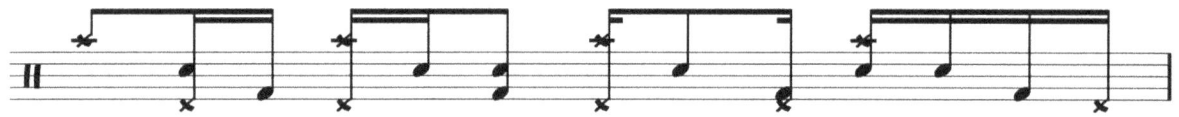

118

7 AGAINST 4
VARIATION 4

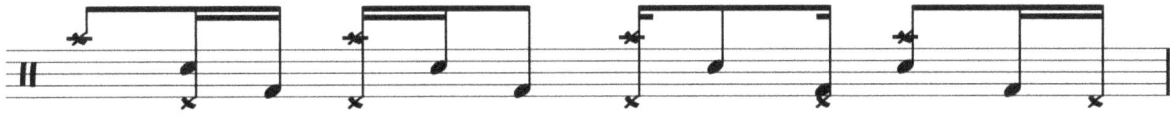

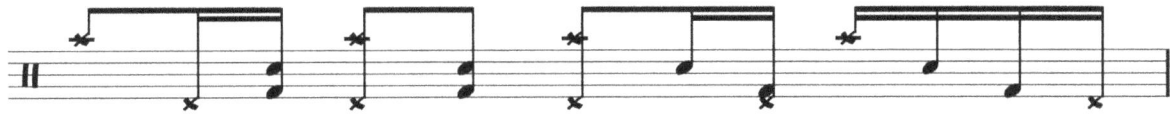

119

## Tuplet Subdivision

The tuplet ostinatos from the three-note variations are utilized here. As with the previous exercise, apply the same variations mentioned at the beginning of the section to these exercises.

## Four on the floor variation

2 Against 3

3 Against 3

4 Against 3

5 Against 3

122

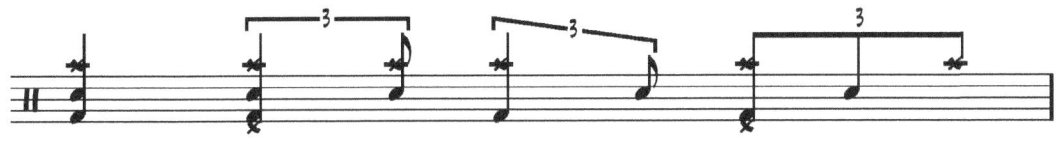

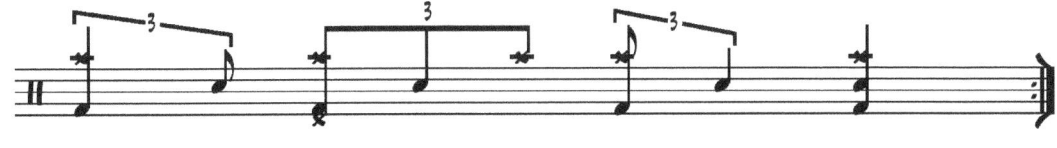

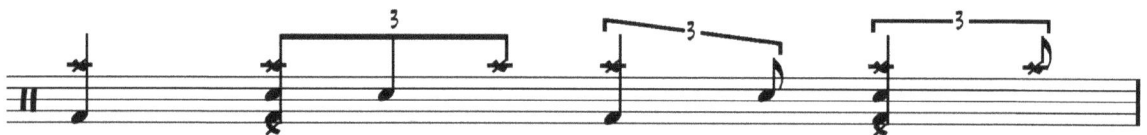

6 AGAINST 3

6 AGAINST 3
VARIATION 2

7 Against 3

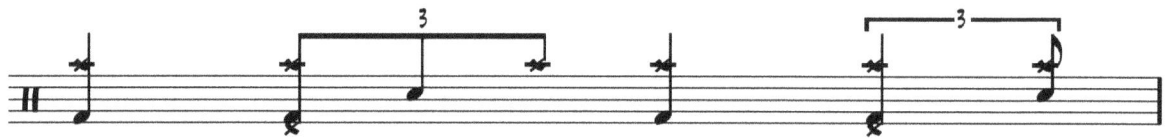

7 AGAINST 3
VARIATION 2

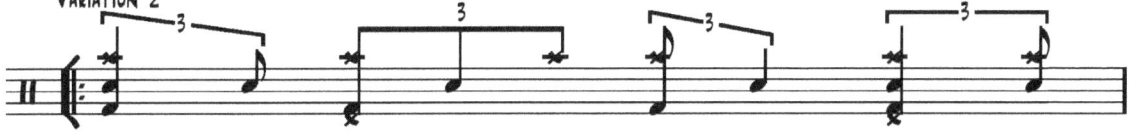

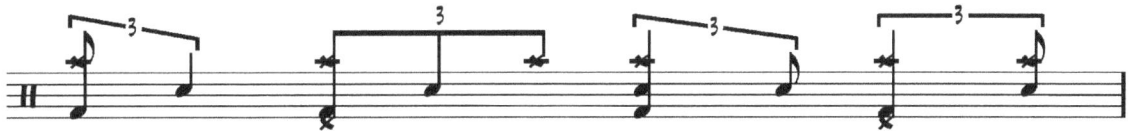

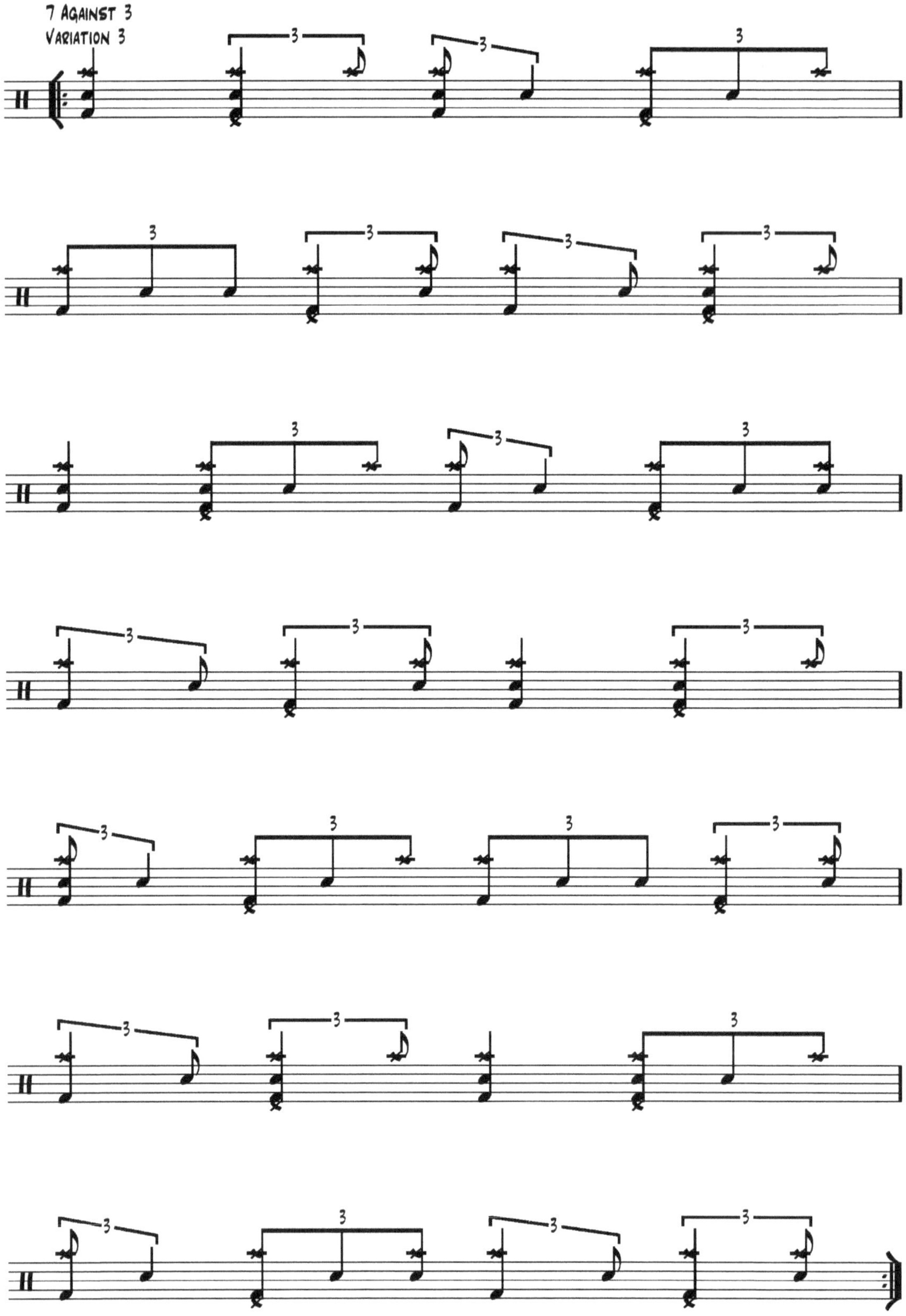
7 Against 3
Variation 3

7 Against 3
Variation 4

## Reggae Variation

2 Against 3

3 Against 3

4 Against 3

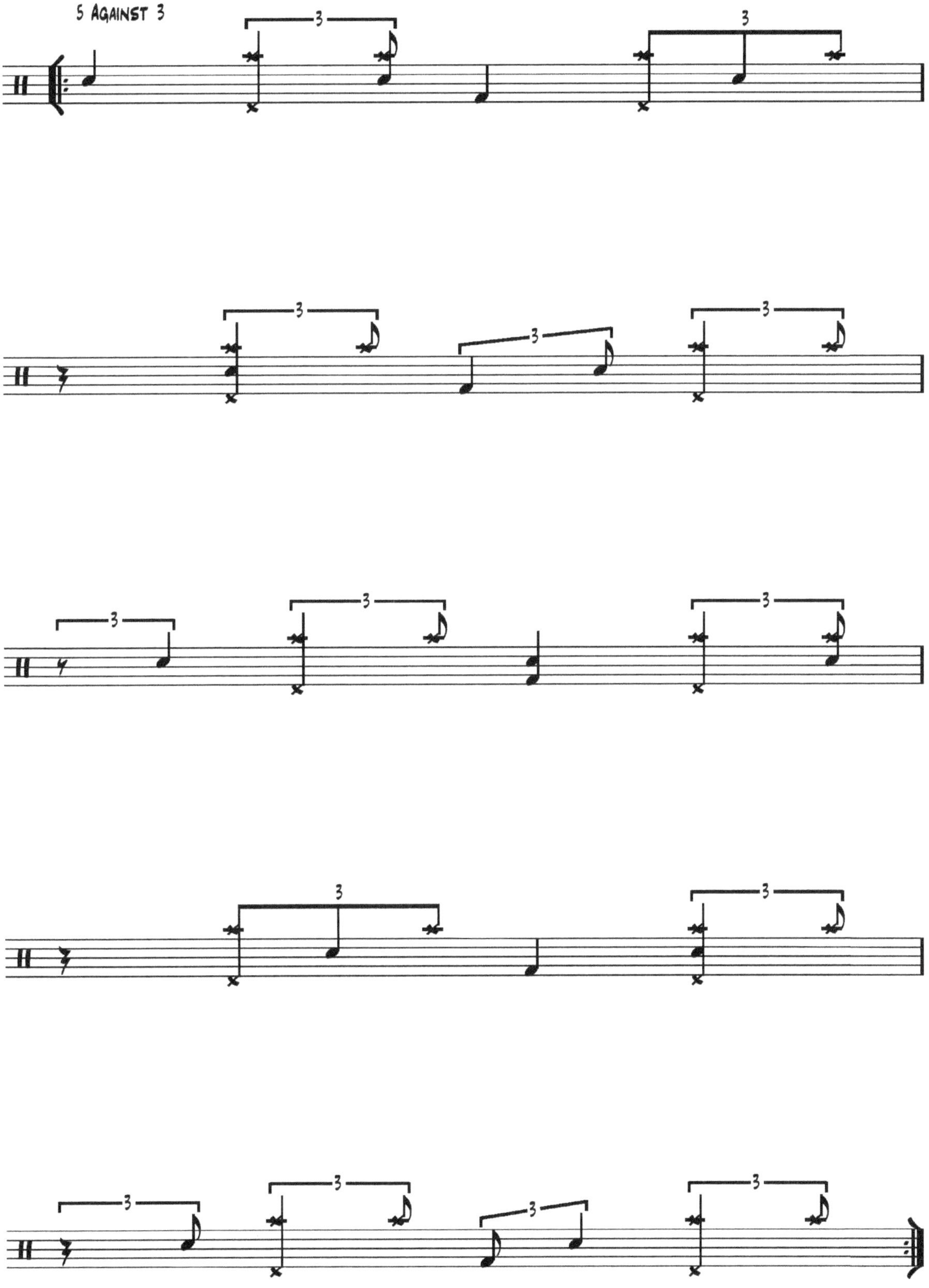
5 Against 3

5 Against 3
Variation 2

5 AGAINST 3
VARIATION 3

133

6 AGAINST 3

6 AGAINST 3
VARIATION 2

7 Against 3

135

7 Against 3
Variation 2

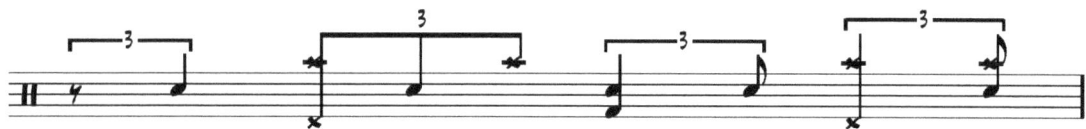

136

7 Against 3
Variation 3

137

138

## Shuffle Variation

2 Against 3

3 Against 3

4 Against 3

5 AGAINST 3
VARIATION 2

141

5 Against 3
Variation 3

142

6 AGAINST 3

6 AGAINST 3
VARIATION 2

143

7 AGAINST 3

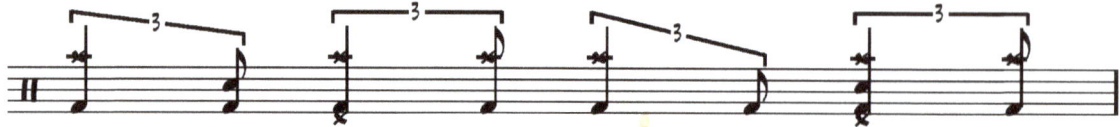

7 AGAINST 3
VARIATION 2

145

7 Against 3
Variation 3

146

7 AGAINST 3
VARIATION 4

www.ingramcontent.com/pod-product-compliance
Lightning Source LLC
Chambersburg PA
CBHW081513040426

42447CB00013B/3214